DISNEY'S

American Frontier #11

TECUMSEH:
ONE NATION FOR HIS
PEOPLE

A Historical Novel

by Gina Ingoglia

Illustrations by Charlie Shaw

Cover illustration by Dave Henderson

DISNEY
PRESS

NEW YORK

Look for these other books in the
American Frontier series:

Davy Crockett and the King of the River

Davy Crockett and the Creek Indians

Davy Crockett and the Pirates at Cave-in Rock

Davy Crockett at the Alamo

Johnny Appleseed and the Planting of the West

Davy Crockett and the Highwaymen

Sacajawea and the Journey to the Pacific

Calamity Jane at Fort Sanders

Annie Oakley in the Wild West Extravaganza!

Wild Bill Hickok and the Rebel Raiders

Davy Crockett Meets Death Hug

FIRST EDITION
1 3 5 7 9 10 8 6 4 2

Library of Congress Catalog Card Number: 92-56162
ISBN: 1-56282-490-2/1-56282-489-9 (lib. bdg.)

Consultant: Barbara Sklar Maslekoff, Librarian
Ohioana Library, Columbus, Ohio
Editor, *Ohioana Quarterly*

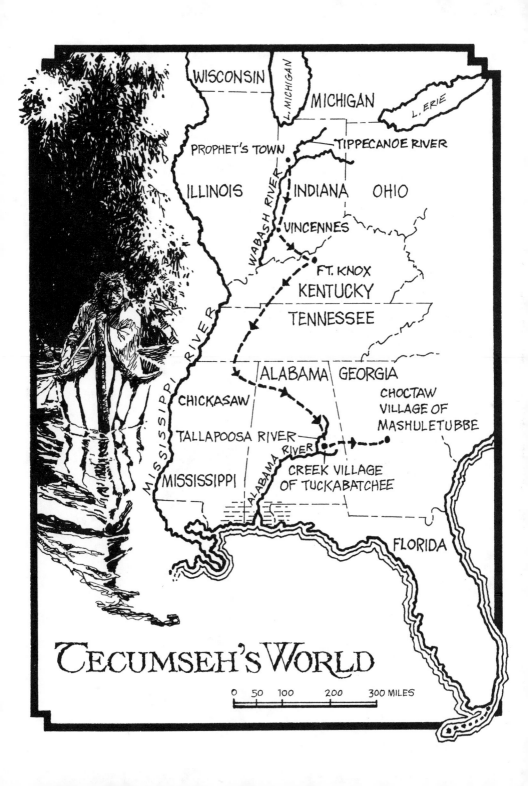

WISCONSIN

L. MICHIGAN

MICHIGAN

L. ERIE

PROPHET'S TOWN

TIPPECANOE RIVER

ILLINOIS

WABASH RIVER

INDIANA

OHIO

VINCENNES

FT. KNOX

KENTUCKY

TENNESSEE

MISSISSIPPI RIVER

ALABAMA GEORGIA

CHICKASAW

CHOCTAW
VILLAGE OF
MASHULETUBBE

TALLAPOOSA RIVER

ALABAMA RIVER

CREEK VILLAGE
OF TUCKABATCHEE

MISSISSIPPI

FLORIDA

TECUMSEH'S WORLD

0   50   100   200   300 MILES

CHAPTER 1

The four hundred young men had been paddling downstream on the Wabash River for more than a week. The hot August sun beat down mercilessly on their backs. It had been a very long trip, and they were tired.

Their chief, Tecumseh, rode in the lead canoe. His otter-pelt headdress was plain except for a single feather. His cousin, Black Feather, sat beside him. His headdress of long porcupine hairs fanned out like a brush.

"Look ahead, Cousin," said Tecumseh. A wooden fort rose high on the banks above the river. "We are drawing close to Fort Knox."

Black Feather shaded his eyes against the glare of the sun. A line of soldiers was standing along the bluff.

"The soldiers are curious," Tecumseh said. "Some are looking at us through their spyglasses."

The canoes glided downriver past the fort.

"How young and eager they appear," he told his cousin. "Ready to fight. And down here are my own brave warriors, also young, ready to defend their land—and to die."

Black Feather was startled. "You are not expecting a battle *now!*" he said.

Tecumseh shook his head. "Of course not," he replied. "Now we are on a mission of peace to see Governor Harrison. But if he does not change his mind about the new treaty, then soon there will be war!"

One of the braves paddling in the rear of the long canoe leaned close to a comrade.

"We should make war now," he muttered. "Why wait until the white men are prepared to fight us?"

Tecumseh spun in his seat and glared at the young man.

"Can you speak as you do—and still be one of us?" Tecumseh roared.

The warrior lowered his head. He might have known Tecumseh would overhear him. It was said the man had the ears of a fox.

Tecumseh searched the faces of the other men, who were silently paddling. "Who else is as eager to spill his blood?" he demanded. "Speak! Let me hear you!"

No one dared to look at Tecumseh. When their chief was angry, his eyes could make the bravest warrior afraid.

"I did not need you all on this trip," Tecumseh told them. "But you men from northern tribes wanted to see this land the white men call Indiana. Now I hear one man wishing to turn your trip of pleasure into a warring party!"

Tecumseh pointed up to Fort Knox. "Why do those white men not shoot?" he asked. "From their place of advantage, they could destroy us with their bullets. No, they hold their fire because they have been told our mission is one of peace!"

Tecumseh turned his back to his men and stared straight ahead. Black Feather gently touched his cousin's deerskin sleeve.

"That brave is young and inexperienced, Tecumseh," he said. "It's natural for a strong brave to want to show his strength."

Tecumseh turned to Black Feather. "He should know better! He is a member of my federation and knows I want peace. Our only hope for peace is that if the governor feels the strength of the federation, he will understand that if he pushes us, we will push back with strength equal to his. If we must fight, however, we have to wait. The federation is still weak. If we fight in a war before the federation is strong, we will be driven back."

"Do you think the southern tribes will join with us?" asked Black Feather.

"If they do not, we are lost," answered Tecumseh. "Without them, we will not be able to hold back the American army. But with our southern brothers, our defense will be strong—stretching from the northern lands near the Great Lakes down to the southlands the white men have named Alabama and Georgia."

"I hear that far to the west, the land ends and never-ending waters begin," said Black Feather. "If the white men have their way, they will push our people more and more west until all of us drop off into those waters— never to be seen again!"

"I hope you are getting ready to swim!" Tecumseh responded.

Both men laughed. Black Feather was relieved that his cousin could still make jokes.

Tecumseh gestured toward the old sycamores that shaded the river's edge. "Do you remember when we were boys, we climbed those trees and fished with our fathers from the shore?

"For hundreds of years the Shawnee have wandered these lands," he continued. "How can we and those of other tribes be forced to live forever anywhere else? This land gives us life! Here, we celebrate our successful hunts in the spring and plentiful harvests in the fall."

Tecumseh scanned the countryside that stretched away from the river. "Beneath those grasses, our ancestors rest," he said. "The white men will not honor our dead. The bones of our sacred elders will be trod upon by the feet of uncaring strangers!"

Thunder sounded in the distance, and soon gray clouds blocked the sun. The water lost its sparkle, and fat drops of rain spattered on the men's backs.

"The thunderbirds are flapping their wings," said Black Feather. "I hope when their eyes begin to flash, we will be off this river!"

Tecumseh studied the darkening sky.

"Now is not a good time to meet," he decided. "Men cannot easily make peace upon the earth while thunderbirds—the patrons of war and gatekeepers of heaven—wage a battle."

"Still, the storm is a good sign," said Black Feather. "The war in the sky will make the air clean and pure. That is a favorable atmosphere for a council of peace."

"After we set up camp, I wish you to take a message to the governor," Tecumseh told his cousin. "Tell him I will not meet with him until the rains stop."

Tecumseh spotted a grassy knoll beside the river. On its crest, a large brick house stood next to a grove of chestnut trees.

"It is the dwelling of Governor William Henry Harrison," Tecumseh told Black Feather. "Two boys are climbing a tree. Perhaps they are the governor's sons."

CHAPTER 2

Seven-year-old John Scott Harrison climbed higher for a better view up the Wabash River. He stretched his arm around the rough trunk and felt his jacket rip. Straddling a sturdy limb, he wiped his hands on his breeches and pulled up his grimy silk stockings. He bent his head, retied his hair at the back of his neck, and noticed he'd lost a buckle from one of his shoes.

"See anything yet?" called out his younger brother, Benjamin, perched on a branch several feet below. They'd been watching for the canoes all day.

John Scott shook his head.

"I hear thunder," said Benjamin, sounding disappointed. "If it's raining, maybe they won't come today."

"Don't be silly," said John Scott. "Rain doesn't bother Indians." Suddenly the flotilla glided into view. "I can see them! Look at them all! Quick, go tell Father!"

Benjamin scrambled down from the tree. As the boy raced across the lawn, a tall, thin man opened the front door of the mansion. Governor William Henry Harrison crossed the wide portico and stepped onto the lawn.

"Father, the Indians are coming!" Benjamin shouted. "A whole bunch of 'em!"

His nine-year-old brother, William, darted out of the mansion, waving a shiny brass tube in the air. "I've got John Cleves's telescope," he announced. "I found it in his room." He ran to the edge of the bluff and put the telescope to his eye.

"Maybe I can find Tecumseh's brother, the one they call the Prophet," he said, peering hard into the lens. "Father says he's only got one eye!"

Governor Harrison overheard his son. "The Prophet isn't coming," the governor told his son.

At that moment a man wearing a black three-cornered hat crossed the lawn and joined them. He was Joseph Barron, the governor's chief adviser on Indian affairs.

"Good heavens, there are hundreds of them!" Barron exclaimed. "When Tecumseh asked if he might take along some extra men, I never dreamed he meant so many. I hope the citizens of Vincennes won't worry they'll be attacked! Perhaps I should call a meeting with the city elders."

"I don't think that's necessary," said the governor. "We've had notices posted in town announcing Tecumseh's arrival. Everyone will believe we expected these great numbers all along."

"Look, Father," William said, holding up the telescope. "The braves are wearing stripes of red paint near their eyes. And they have silver earrings. Some of them even have rings in their noses!"

The governor peered through the lens. "Joseph, which one is Tecumseh?" he asked.

"The man in the lead canoe wearing a deerskin shirt and red leggings," answered Barron. "He wears the single tail feather of a golden eagle in his headdress. It can be worn only by a chief."

"And the man next to him?" Harrison asked.

"That would be his cousin Black Feather," said Barron. "He and I serve similar posts—advisers to our chiefs!"

Harrison laughed and returned the telescope to his son. "Thank you, William," he said, handing back the telescope. "Let your brothers have a look."

He took Barron's arm and steered him toward a private clearing. "I want you to alert the militia. With all these braves, there's a real danger of attack. Their camp must be under constant surveillance. Joseph, you are *certain* it's Tecumseh I should be meeting and not his brother, Tenskwatawa, the one they call the Prophet?"

Joseph Barron's shoulders slumped. He'd been through this with the governor many times.

"Sir," he explained, "when I went to Prophet's Town to arrange this conference for you, Tenskwatawa threatened to kill me on the spot! The man's a hothead. He hates all white men. Luckily for me, Tecumseh stepped in and dismissed his brother from our meeting. He said he wanted to speak with you. Believe me, Governor, Tecumseh is the one you want to see! The federation is his idea."

"This Prophet, however, has a great following," said Harrison. "Many Indians think he's a great shaman, a holy man, chosen by the Great Spirit to lead them. Their headquarters is even named for him."

"I believe he named the headquarters himself," said Barron. "The Prophet is also vain."

"But the Prophet can't be wholly a fool," the governor pointed out. "He managed to outfox me once— making *me* appear the foolish one!"

Barron tried not to smile. "Yes, sir," he agreed, "that was indeed an unfortunate coincidence. He was clever. When you challenged him to perform a miracle, he appeared to do so!"

"How that lucky rascal knew there'd be an eclipse of the sun, I'll never know!" Harrison sighed, and the smile disappeared from his face. "Now this 'miracle man' has more followers than ever. When he tells the

Indian people to join Tecumseh's federation, they listen to him!"

A strong breeze swept across the lawn. In seconds, it was pouring. The two men strode toward the house, and Governor Harrison waved for his sons to follow. Just as they all reached the portico, a deafening thunderclap rattled the windows of the governor's mansion.

Downriver, at the far edge of Vincennes, Tecumseh ordered his men to pull the elm-bark canoes ashore. On an open windy field lashed with rain, the warriors hastily erected buffalo-hide tepees. Then, at last, after traveling two hundred miles, they rested.

CHAPTER 3

The late summer storm rumbled around Vincennes for the next two days. At sunup on the third morning, Tecumseh stepped out of the tepee that he shared with Black Feather.

Studying the brightening sky, he called to his cousin. "Stop dreaming in there and come out!"

Black Feather stuck his head out of the tepee. "Has something happened?" he asked.

Tecumseh smiled. "Yes, the thunderbirds have made peace with one another," he said. "Now we can meet with Governor Harrison. I would like you to carry that word to him."

Tecumseh crossed a field and entered a small grove of hickory trees. Turning to face the rising sun, he closed his eyes and breathed deeply. "May the white chief see the wrongs of his ways," he prayed. With his eyes still closed and the songs of waking birds in his ears, he spoke aloud to the Great Spirit.

Governor Harrison opened the indoor shutters that framed the tall windows of the council chamber. The morning sun gleamed on the yellow poplar floor and brightened the patterns in the carpet.

Joseph Barron knocked softly on the door and entered the room. "Good news, Governor," he announced. "Black Feather has just brought word that the council can now be held."

"It's strange that Tecumseh was so put off by meeting in stormy weather," said the governor. "We'll be meeting inside. What does it matter what's going on outdoors?"

Governor Harrison seated himself at a large, round table in the middle of the room and gestured for Barron to join him.

"President Madison is very concerned that this council go well," Harrison said. "He's worried about the strong support Tecumseh and Tenskwatawa are getting. In just one year this federation—the idea of creating a united Indian nation—has found a great deal of support up north. Many of the Great Lakes tribes are already behind them: the Sauk, the Fox, and the Ojibwa. And the Menominee as well."

Joseph Barron nodded slowly and sighed. "And

don't overlook the Winnebago and many of the Potawatomi," he added. "Tecumseh's also traveled south to see
the Choctaw, the Chickasaw, and the Creek. . . ."

Harrison frowned. "He'll have trouble getting the
southern tribes to join him," he said. "They have good
relations with us. Why should they want to go to war?"

"Sir," Barron tried to explain, "Tecumseh has told
me he does not want to go to war. He's eager to make
peace. But he stated firmly that, *first*, you would have to
agree to end the treaty of Fort Wayne.

"Sir," Barron suggested, "you are governor of the
Northwest Territory, one of the most influential men in
the United States. Can't you convince the president to
abandon the new treaty? Can't we go back to the old
boundary terms we signed with the Indians fifteen years
ago?"

"No, we cannot!" stated Governor Harrison. "The
new treaty gives us precious land that we need. If the
United States is to grow and prosper, we have to have
that land. Bear in mind, the treaty of Fort Wayne was
signed by Indian chiefs who were *willing* to sell us that
land!"

"Tecumseh believes that you forced the chiefs into
it," Barron pointed out.

Governor Harrison ignored this remark.

"My friend," he said to Barron, "I want peace as
much as any man. To accomplish this, I must make

Tecumseh see that his foolhardy notion of an Indian federation will never work. We're much too strong for them!

"Your position as my interpreter is critical, Joseph. You must convey to Tecumseh *exactly* what I am trying to say."

"If I may remind you, sir," said Joseph Barron, "Tecumseh speaks fluent English. You will not have trouble making yourself understood to him."

"I find that hard to believe," said Governor Harrison. "Where was he educated?"

"There's a most interesting story behind that," Barron explained. "It's said that Tecumseh was close friends with an ex–Indian fighter by the name of James Galloway. He lived near the Shawnee village. Galloway's teenage daughter, Rebecca, and Tecumseh fell in love! She taught him English and read aloud plays by Shakespeare. Hamlet was one of his favorite characters. Tecumseh was fascinated by European history. One of his heroes is supposed to be Alexander the Great!"

Governor Harrison grinned. "So that's where he got his grand ideas of leading a vast army!" he exclaimed.

"Wait, there's more," said Barron. "It's also rumored that Tecumseh actually *proposed marriage* to Miss Galloway! She accepted, but only if Tecumseh would give up his life as a Shawnee and live as a white man. He refused, but I hear it nearly broke his heart."

The governor raised his eyebrows in amazement. "What an incredible story!" He rose from his chair and paced up and down the room, thinking.

"Many tribes that Tecumseh wishes to unite are bitter enemies," he said at last to Barron. "Do you believe that he can convince them to mend their differences and join together to fight as one?"

"From the time he was a boy," Barron said, "Tecumseh has been a leader. As a warrior he has shown great courage in battle. His men respect him, and of more importance, so do many of his enemies! Tecumseh is known for his fairness. He's gifted with other qualities you might not expect—he's a talented orator, and, I know from my own experience, he's very witty!"

"What you are saying is," concluded Governor Harrison, "Tecumseh can be a real danger to us."

"Yes," said Joseph Barron. "My advice is to choose your words carefully. He will be ready—and able—to pounce on each one!"

They stepped out into the hallway and stopped short.

"Watch out, Father!" cried a voice from the staircase. John Scott and Benjamin slid off the winding banister and collided in a heap on the polished floor.

"Good heavens," said the governor, helping John

Scott to his feet. He turned to Benjamin, who had landed beneath his brother. "Are you all right?"

"I'm fine, Father," said Benjamin, brushing off his jacket. "I guess we were too close together."

"We're all taking our lessons in the parlor with Mother this morning," explained John Scott. "We want to see Tecumseh and his men when they come to the meeting!"

Governor Harrison peered into the parlor. His oldest children, fifteen-year-old Betsy and twelve-year-old John Cleves, were sitting with open books at a large table.

Just then Mrs. Harrison arrived with Lucy, who was three, and young William at her side. She greeted Joseph Barron.

"Anna, for heaven's sake," complained Governor Harrison. "This is a very important council. The children mustn't—"

"Don't worry, William," she said. "When Tecumseh arrives, the children will just look out the window to see him. You will never know there was a child in the house."

"You'll see, Father," said Benjamin. "We'll be quiet as mice."

CHAPTER 4

Governor Harrison, followed by Joseph Barron, walked out onto the mansion's spacious portico. A squad of twelve soldiers in full-dress uniform snapped to attention and saluted.

Prominent civilians, including several justices of the territorial supreme court, were also there, gathered in small clusters and chatting excitedly. Winamac, a Potawatomi chief, stood almost hidden behind a wooden pillar. He had his back to the others and was looking off into the distance.

With the governor's arrival, conversation stopped, and one by one each man shook hands with him.

A soldier walked up and clicked his heels. "Chief Tecumseh has arrived at the foot of the hill, sir," he said.

"Thank you," Governor Harrison replied. He looked across the sloping lawn and could see Tecumseh approaching, accompanied by an honor guard of thirty or more braves.

Suddenly Governor Harrison frowned and turned to Joseph Barron. "Why are they stopping?" he asked. Barron shrugged. "Go see if there's a problem." Barron nodded and walked across the lawn. He spoke with Tecumseh a moment or two and then returned to the governor's side.

"Tecumseh says he does not wish to meet in the house," Barron reported. "He would like to meet outdoors in the fresh air."

Governor Harrison narrowed his eyes. Then he smiled to himself. "The man is a fox," he said. "By asking for this change, he's controlling the council right from the start. Tell him it is fine with me, Joseph. I will tell the others to move across to the lawn."

Several minutes later, both leaders met face-to-face.

"I heartily agree with your suggestion," the governor told Tecumseh, shaking his hand. "It will be more pleasant to sit outdoors. I will order chairs and benches for your comfort. Our Great White Father in Washington wishes you to be shown every courtesy."

"*Our* father? Your President Madison is not my father," Tecumseh said. He pointed to the sky. "The Great Spirit above is my father. The earth is my mother. And upon my mother's breast I will recline."

Tecumseh walked to a shady spot and positioned

himself, at ease, on the grass. He signaled for his men to accompany him and waited expectantly for Governor Harrison.

The governor sighed. "I think we'd better join him," he said quietly to Joseph Barron. "Tell the others to gather around as best they can." He sat down next to the chief and smiled. "Now," he said, "I trust we can begin."

Tecumseh smiled back in agreement.

"Your people have not kept their word to my people. Fifteen years ago your General Wayne defeated us in the Battle of Fallen Timbers. The next spring in Greenville, men from twelve tribes—nearly one thousand strong— met with you in a meeting of peace. They gave you almost two-thirds of our land, what you now call Ohio, along with land in Indiana and Michigan. In return you promised to take no more of our land and to leave us in peace."

"Excuse me, my friend, I must interrupt you," said Governor Harrison. "The United States government *bought* the land from your people. You did not give it to us."

"They could not help themselves," Tecumseh said. "They were defeated men. They sold it to you for twenty thousand dollars. Your government also was to provide them with an additional sum of money—less than ten thousand dollars—each year."

He rose to his feet. Governor Harrison immediately did the same.

"Do you think that was fair payment for the lands that our people had lived on for thousands of years?" Tecumseh asked. "Lands that provide us with food for our bellies and a home for raising our young?" He shook his head. "No it was not! We did it to make peace."

"The United States wishes to make peace, too," said Governor Harrison. "You must believe this."

"For the white man," Tecumseh said, " 'making peace' means taking away my people's land without a battle!"

He glared at Governor Harrison. "Last September, less than one year ago," he said, "you yourself, Governor, signed a new treaty at Fort Wayne, and you took away even more of our land. *Three million acres!* This time, it included much of my own tribe's precious hunting territory—"

"Chief Tecumseh," Harrison pointed out, "the new treaty was signed by chiefs with legitimate claims along the Wabash. The Delaware were represented. Little Turtle signed for the Miami and Chief Winamac for a good number of Potawatomi."

"I do not agree that their claims to this land were legitimate," Tecumseh countered.

Tecumseh shook his head. "Besides, Little Turtle

was ill. He is too ill to make good judgments. As for the rest of the chiefs," he said, glancing hatefully at Winamac, "they are fools. No tribe has a right to sell land even to each other, much less to strangers. The earth cannot be owned. No one can own a creation of the Great Spirit!

"*Sell* the earth?" he cried, raising his voice. "Why not sell the air, the clouds, and the great sea, as well as the land? Did not the Great Spirit make them all for the use of his children?"

"Chief," said Governor Harrison, "surely all the lands covered by the treaty don't belong to your Shawnee tribe."

Tecumseh opened his arms wide. "All the land— everywhere—belongs to every tribe! If you do not give back the land," he vowed, "I will kill the chiefs that sold it. I tell you this because I am authorized to do this by their tribes—I am now the chief of them all!"

At this Winamac snorted.

"Who are you to mock me?" Tecumseh roared. "You, who are a traitor!" He raised a clenched fist in the air.

Winamac ducked behind a tree and reached inside his belt.

"He has a gun!" cried out one of Harrison's officials.

Governor Harrison quickly motioned to his soldiers.

"Disarm that man," he ordered. "And lead him away."

"Do not bother!" Tecumseh shouted to the soldiers as they took hold of Winamac. "That coward hurts men only behind their backs. He does not have the courage to shoot me!"

He boldly confronted the Potawatomi chief.

"Shoot if you dare," he challenged. "And when you miss your mark, I will end your life with my hands alone!"

Black Feather reached out to pull him back.

Tecumseh's voice trembled with rage. "Do not touch me!" Tecumseh roared.

Black Feather withdrew his hand at once. It was the first time he'd seen Tecumseh behave badly. And never before had his cousin been rude to him.

Governor Harrison, his face flushed with anger, intervened. "We will have no violence here!" he told Tecumseh. "Your actions are inexcusable. I will talk no more under these conditions."

Not giving Tecumseh the chance to respond, Governor Harrison turned his back to him and walked away. The council of peace was over.

CHAPTER 5

Standing with his head held high, Tecumseh watched Governor Harrison return to the mansion. Then, without a word to Black Feather, he strode back to camp.

Late that night in their tent, Tecumseh sat with his face in his hands. After a long while, he raised his head. "I have disgraced myself, Black Feather," he said. "Worse, I have disgraced my people. I am a Shawnee chief, a position of honor. It is my duty to control my feelings. And, Cousin, I will never forgive myself for speaking to you as I did."

"Tecumseh," Black Feather said quietly, "it is not worth the time to think about it. I know your true feelings for me. Tell me why you became so enraged at Winamac. Was it because he scorned your power?"

"I do not care what that worthless man thinks of me," answered Tecumseh. "No, it was because he laughed. I could not bear to hear laughter coming from such a man, a man whose actions will bring tears to our people.

"Winamac and those chiefs who signed the treaty— how can they believe the white man's promises? This new treaty is to be the first of many. Each one will be torn up with a new treaty to take its place.

"Cousin, the council must go on," he continued. "We must not lose this opportunity for peace. I want you to take a message to the governor's dwelling. Say it is my great desire that Governor Harrison agrees to resume the meeting."

Later that day Tecumseh faced Governor Harrison for the second time and offered him his hand.

"Before we begin, Governor," he said, "I must apologize for my behavior yesterday. It was unforgivable."

Governor Harrison shook the chief's hand. "All of us have moments we'd rather forget," he said quietly.

"It is my hope," said Tecumseh, "that today we will, as my people say, follow the white path of peace and not take the red road to war."

Governor Harrison looked surprised. "We are not here to talk of war. This is a council of peace."

"Let us hope that that will be so," said Tecumseh.

But by late afternoon, no new agreement had been reached.

"Before we part," Governor Harrison said to Tecumseh, "let me pose a question to you: Will you allow my surveyors, men who make maps, to look over the three million acres—the land obtained by the new treaty?"

Tecumseh's mood was grave. He understood that with the white man, once lines are drawn on a piece of paper, boundaries become permanent. Tecumseh would not allow this. He would not permit Indian territory to be divided, even on paper. "If that happens, it will be difficult for me to remain your friend," said Tecumseh. "Should your surveyors enter those lands, I assure you I will take action against them."

With heavy hearts, Tecumseh and Governor Harrison parted.

Tecumseh and his braves remained at Vincennes for several more days. On the day before they were to return home to Tippecanoe, Governor Harrison paid a visit to Tecumseh's camp.

"Chief Tecumseh," he said, "I thought we might speak one last time."

Tecumseh smiled and extended his hand to the governor.

"There is a place for us to sit," he said, gesturing to a bench close by.

"I have considered your demands and your objections

to my government's policies," Harrison said, seating himself on the bench. "I will send them to President Madison."

"If it be so," said Tecumseh, sitting next to him, "that your chief will decide this matter, then I hope the Great Spirit will put some sense in his head and convince him to give up this land. But President Madison may not care—he is so far off in Washington. He can sit in his town and drink wine while you and I have to fight it out!"

"Chief Tecumseh," said Harrison, "I must confess something to you. I believe there is little chance that the white chief will end the new treaty."

As the two men were talking, the governor became aware that Tecumseh kept moving closer to him. Harrison shifted over to give Tecumseh more room. Tecumseh moved closer again. Once more, the governor retreated.

"Chief," he asked, "are you trying to knock me off this bench?"

Tecumseh gave a mirthless laugh. "Now you know how my people feel—when your settlers come in and push us off our land!"

Tecumseh rose and walked a little distance away, keeping his back to the other man. Governor Harrison stood but did not follow. Several minutes passed. Then the chief turned and walked back.

"It is my turn now," Tecumseh said, "to reveal something to you. I have spoken like a brother to all the tribal nations between the Great Lakes and the Gulf of Mexico and as far west as the prairie country of the Iowa and Sioux. Many of their warriors have joined my federation and are now living in my headquarters up in Prophet's Town. One day soon I will travel again to the tribes in the South.

"Let us talk about the British for a moment," he said. "Since the revolutionary war, their army remains up in Canada. I know that they pose a threat to your seaports. I know the United States may very well go to war with them.

"In the past, I made a promise. I said if the white men honored the boundary of the old treaty drawn up fifteen years ago, my people would keep the peace." Tecumseh pointed his finger, shaking it as he spoke. "But now you feel sure that President Madison will keep the boundary of the new treaty. If this becomes true, I will go to Canada to see the British. I will gain their support, and they will get mine. It is a promise!"

Governor Harrison wasn't shocked by this news. His spies had informed him of Tecumseh's desire to join with the British. An alliance between the Indians and the British was a real danger that had troubled the Americans.

But why is he telling me this? Harrison wondered.

Tecumseh's a shrewd man who's never been known for disclosing his plans prematurely. Has he chosen his words wisely? Or is he, perhaps, just being boastful and foolish?

The governor remembered something Joseph Barron had once told him. "The Shawnee are each named for a certain group of animals—horses, birds, bears, and so on. Those names are called their *unsomas*—good luck symbols to guide and bless them throughout their lives.

"Tecumseh is a Cat Man. But his name means more than one thing," Joseph had told him. "It means 'the panther who crouches, lying in wait'; it also means 'the shooting star, which causes wonder.' The best way I can translate it is, 'a magical panther from the heavens.' "

Joseph had added a warning. "Tecumseh is well named," he cautioned. "A panther is not easily trapped. It recognizes danger even when that danger is still distant. It is clever and plans its moves well."

Harrison decided that Tecumseh had indeed chosen his words carefully. Now it was his turn to choose his own.

"Chief Tecumseh," said Harrison, "you claim this land should belong only to your people. But remember, at one time *no* people were living here. Your people came here from somewhere else and claimed it. Why should this whole continent be yours alone?"

Tecumseh nodded. "You are right, it was not always our land," he said. "But the white men do not seem to understand something very important—land belongs to the first people who find it!

"I hope you can persuade President Madison to see my position," continued Tecumseh, extending his right hand to the governor.

The men shook hands.

"I see you have accepted one custom of the white man," said Governor Harrison, looking at their clasped hands.

Tecumseh smiled. "It is you who have accepted our courtesy, Governor," he said. "For centuries Shawnee men have shaken hands in friendship."

"I see," said Governor Harrison, making himself return the smile. "That is very interesting." Once again Tecumseh had had a ready answer.

Both men realized all that could be said had been spoken. Their council of peace was over.

CHAPTER 6

At dawn the next morning Tecumseh and his men began the long journey home.

For several days they paddled north far up the Wabash River. Where the waters divided, they took the left fork called the Tippecanoe River. There lay Prophet's Town. Fifteen hundred members of the federation lived in dwellings spaced along the riverbank.

It had rained hard the night before, and the day was chilly.

"It is good to be back," said Black Feather, climbing out of the canoe. Tecumseh stretched his arms above his head and breathed in the misty air. He bent his right knee and winced.

"Your knee is stiff again?" asked his cousin.

"Yes," said Tecumseh. "It will be better after I walk on it. I will leave you in charge here while I find my brother."

Tecumseh felt disgusted as he limped to shore. For months his knee had given him no trouble. Now the pain was back. It had been this way since his nineteenth summer. Would this bad leg *never* be right? For twenty-three long years he had put up with this pain. He remembered the day he had fallen, thrown from his horse in the middle of a hunt. Even now he could feel the pain as if it were only yesterday.

To think of that time hurt his heart as well. The next year, Cheesekau, his older brother, had died the honorable death of a warrior. Before the battle, Cheesekau had had a vision. "I will die at noon," he had predicted. Early the next morning he had been shot in the face by a white man. And when the sun was directly overhead, he had died.

Tecumseh wandered past the empty council house and the House of Strangers. The House of Strangers was always open to receive visiting pilgrims. Ever since word had spread that his brother had darkened the sun, hundreds had made the pilgrimage to the village to receive the Prophet's blessing.

Tecumseh followed the sound of voices coming from the Tabernacle. He quietly entered the building and stood at the back of the crowded room.

The Prophet was preaching to a crowd of about fifty people who shouted prayers and shook strings of sacred white beans that the holy man had blessed.

"You must believe this," Tenskwatawa told them. "Five years ago I was very sick, and everybody thought I would die. But, not so. My soul was taken from my body. A pair of spirits took me to a place beyond the sky, where I was presented to the Master of Life. Then they brought me back to earth to give His message to you."

As Tecumseh listened, he remembered the man his brother had been before being stricken by that strange illness. He had been a man of disgrace, a troublemaker, one who held no one's respect. Then, in the middle of his sickness, he had awakened, as from a trance, announcing that he was changed. He desired a new name. He wanted to be called Tenskwatawa—"Open Door." It was then that he began his new life as a preacher and holy man.

"Use nothing of the white man's," Tenskwatawa warned the assembly. "Use no cloth made by him. Use no flint or steel as fire starters. You must rub sticks together instead. Hunt only with bows and arrows, but you may fight with guns in battle. And in your lodges, you must keep a fire burning for the Master of Life.

"If you believe in me," Tenskwatawa cried, "I will cause the white man's bullets to bounce harmlessly from your chests. You will be invisible to your enemies!"

Tecumseh frowned. His brother must not tell such lies!

The Prophet pointed to his empty eye socket. "I have but one eye," he said, "but still I see clearly. . . ."

Tecumseh remembered the day long ago when his younger brother had lost his eye while playing carelessly with a bow and arrow. Cheesekau had come running and carried him screaming to the shaman's lodge. "You must not cry like this," the shaman had scolded. "A Shawnee boy must not show pain if he wants to become a brave warrior. . . ."

"Together as one nation," Tenskwatawa shouted, "we will defeat the white man!" He raised his fist and shook a string of beans. "Now, shake hands with the Prophet!" he called out. "Show me that you are with us!"

The crowd shouted back, shaking their bean strings in the air. Walking in little groups, they strolled toward the door. Tecumseh stepped out of the shadows and stopped Tenskwatawa.

"Ah, Brother," said the Prophet. "You are back. I hope that you did well at the council of peace?"

"It did not go very well," said Tecumseh. "Governor Harrison will convey our demands to the white chief in Washington. Do not hold much hope he will grant them."

"Ha!" snapped Tenskwatawa. "I knew I should have gone. Do not forget, the governor had invited me. He would have listened to *me!*"

"You!" said Tecumseh. "When Joseph Barron came

to visit, you called him an American spy. Then you told him to look down at the ground at his feet, telling him it would be his grave!"

Tenskwatawa turned to leave. "I am not finished, my brother," Tecumseh said, grabbing his arm. "You must not tell our followers that you can make their bodies invisible and make harmless the bullets of white men."

"Why not?" asked Tenskwatawa. "If they think that, they will follow us into battle."

Tecumseh said firmly, "I do not want men fighting for us believing they cannot be killed."

Tenskwatawa twisted his arm from Tecumseh's grasp. "You forget, my older brother," he said. "Many of our followers came here because of *me*—not you! I will tell them what I please."

The Prophet smiled. "Word has come to me about Main Poc, the old Potawatomi chief," he said.

Tecumseh quickly drew in his breath. Main Poc, one of the first to join the federation, was a troublemaker.

"What has he done?" he asked.

"While you were away, he made a raid against the white settlers," said Tenskwatawa. "He has killed six of them. Then some of his braves went south. They crossed the Mississippi River and ambushed several Osage braves and killed them as well."

Tecumseh threw his head back and squeezed his eyes shut. Now there is no hope that I can convince the

Osage to join with us, he thought. How could Main Poc have done such a thing!

Tecumseh looked at Tenskwatawa, who was still smiling. "Are you happy this has happened?" he demanded.

"No, I am not happy about the danger to the federation," the Prophet said calmly. "But I am happy to see that success does not always come to my elder brother."

He pushed Tecumseh aside and went on his way.

Tecumseh walked out of the Tabernacle to a little bluff overlooking the river. It was the place he went to think.

In a little while, Black Feather appeared. "May I join you?"

"You have come at a good time," said Tecumseh. "I need to talk with you. Main Poc has been making raids against the whites. Tenskwatawa seems happy about it! He says he doesn't like to see things always go my way. As if this were about me!"

"You know he is jealous of you," said Black Feather.

"I believe I have made a mistake in joining together with this younger brother," said Tecumseh. "He has been a fool all his life; why should he be different now?"

"Yet after his illness," said Black Feather, "he seemed to change for the better. It seemed like good fortune for the two of you to work together—you to do the planning, and the Prophet to help attract followers to the federation. What makes you have such doubts now?"

"Tenskwatawa is filling the people with lies," Tecumseh explained. "He says he can protect them in battle—by making the white man's bullets harmless!"

"You did not mind when he fooled everyone into thinking he could put out the sun," Black Feather pointed out.

"That was not the same thing," said Tecumseh. "The governor tried to disgrace us in the eyes of our people. If we could both gain support and embarrass Governor Harrison, so much the better!

"But now," Tecumseh said gloomily, "I fear for the federation. Tell me, how can I work with a man who pretends he is God?"

CHAPTER 7

The winter months at Prophet's Town passed peacefully. Every week or so, visiting pilgrims came to listen to the Prophet's holy words, then traveled back to their own villages. After the snows began to fall, no more pilgrims came, and the people of Prophet's Town stayed indoors. The only signs of life were curls of gray smoke from campfires burning in the lodges.

Then the spring thaw awakened the frozen land, and Prophet's Town bustled as new braves arrived, ready to join the federation.

One morning a messenger arrived from Vincennes.

"Governor Harrison wishes to meet with me again," Tecumseh told his cousin.

"Perhaps the white chief in Washington has reached a decision!" said Black Feather.

"We leave for Vincennes at sunrise tomorrow," said Tecumseh, "this time with only twenty-one of my bravest warriors. After my meeting with the governor, we will journey to the southern tribes. They must join the federation. Even if the white chief in Washington gives us our land back today, who is to say he will not take it back tomorrow?

"I would rather leave you here to watch Tenskwatawa," he told Black Feather, "but I need you to interpret the tongues of our southern brothers. While you take charge of the preparations, I will have a word with my brother."

Tecumseh found Tenskwatawa snoring softly beneath a tree.

"What do you want?" asked the Prophet, drowsy with sleep.

"You must make a promise to me," said Tecumseh. "You must keep the peace while I am away. Until the federation is complete and strong, we must not engage in any conflict. Unless, of course, you are attacked. Are you listening to me?"

"Elder Brother," answered the Prophet with a little smile, "I hear everything you say." Then he turned over and went back to sleep.

The meeting in Vincennes was brief. Governor Harrison welcomed Tecumseh and came right to the point.

"As I anticipated, Chief Tecumseh," he reported,

"President Madison will not agree to your demands. The treaty that I signed with the chiefs stands."

Tecumseh was consumed with both grief and anger. So the white settlers were free to push west! He knew there was no argument left. The decision was final. Keeping his emotions hidden, he began to speak.

"I would like to meet with the white chief in Washington," he said. "But first I must travel south. One year ago I told you of these plans. But I make a promise to you. While I am away, my brother in Prophet's Town will keep the peace. Upon my return, I hope with my heart that I will be able to make a permanent peace with your President Madison."

The governor exchanged glances with Joseph Barron. Here, again, Tecumseh was revealing plans that should have been kept secret!

"Chief Tecumseh, when you return from the South," said Governor Harrison, "I shall send word to President Madison. I'm certain he will look forward to meeting with you."

The next day Tecumseh and his men began their journey south on the Wabash River. Like a winding watery serpent, the river wound its way through Indiana down to Kentucky. Some fifty miles downstream from Vincennes, where the Wabash empties into the wide Ohio River, Tecumseh ordered his men to go ashore. They would travel the rest of the trip on land.

That afternoon Tecumseh sat on the riverbank with his cousin. A nightjar sang in a nearby field. The men listened carefully to the bird. It is still too early in the day for a nightjar, Tecumseh thought. There it was again. But not quite! Tecumseh smiled at Black Feather and rose to his feet. He crossed a grassy field and stopped in front of a large bush.

"Come out, Nightjar," Tecumseh said. "Let me take a look at you."

Instead of a brown-and-black spotted bird, a little barefoot boy appeared, clutching a fishnet that bulged with a captured bass. His leggings and buckskin shirt were spattered with mud. He wore a cap of wildcat skin with a small bunch of feathers stuck in the top. The boy was a Shawnee. Tecumseh decided he could not have been more than six or seven summers.

"Your nightjar call is good," said Tecumseh.

The boy looked disappointed. "I was practicing," he said. "But you could tell it wasn't a real nightjar."

"But someday I will not be able to," said Tecumseh. "If you keep on trying, you won't sound so much like a sick bird." He smiled. "Do not look so sad. Your name isn't Croaking Nightjar, is it?"

The little boy threw back his head and laughed. "No," he said with pride, "my name is Swift Fox."

"Well, you see, you were given a good name," said Tecumseh. "Your people must think you will become a clever hunter. Someday you will be fooling everyone with your call of the nightjar. Now, tell me. I would like to buy some horses. Do you know where I might find some?"

"I will take you to our camp," said Swift Fox. "My father has horses. He is away but will return by sundown. He will be proud of the big fish I caught!"

Tecumseh gazed at the smiling boy and saw an image of himself at that age. He'd always tried to make his own father, Puckeshinwa, feel proud of him, his second son. But when he was about the same age as Swift Fox, his father was killed fighting the frontiersmen, those white men his people called the Long Knives.

He would never forget that terrible day: His father and his brother Cheesekau, then fourteen summers old, had fought side by side. After his father had been shot, Cheesekau swam with him across the Ohio River. When they reached the shore, Puckeshinwa died in his arms.

Tecumseh hoped this boy would never have to fight the white men in battle. But without the strength of the federation in place, it was certain the United States Army would take this land. And the boy's father, and perhaps the boy himself, would fight to save it.

Tecumseh called to Black Feather and several warriors, and they followed Swift Fox across the field to his camp.

"Do you remember," Black Feather asked Tecumseh, "when we were boys, how the elders called out to us, never speaking our names, but making sounds like birds and other animals? It made us learn them quickly."

"Yes," said Tecumseh. "You were the best of us at birdcalls—but that's natural—your *unsoma* is a bird. Of course, your mountain lions always sounded like the horned owls!"

"Well, Cat Man," joked Black Feather, "your imitation of the wild goose was more like that of a wildcat in pain!"

Tecumseh put his arm around his cousin's shoulder and laughed.

"There are my father's horses," said Swift Fox. He pointed to a small herd of black animals tethered together.

Tecumseh smiled. "They are fine," he said. He turned to Black Feather. "It will be good for us all to ride on black horses. We will make a fine sight. While I am visiting with the boy's family, you and the men inspect these animals. Make sure they are all healthy."

Swift Fox led Tecumseh to his family's bark-covered *weg-i-wa*, their summer lodge. His mother was sitting on the floor, playing a game with his baby sister.

"There is hot food on the fire," said the boy's mother, getting up to welcome Tecumseh. "Please eat with us."

"*Niawe*—I thank you," said Tecumseh.

The woman scooped spicy corn mush into a bowl and handed it to Tecumseh, with a chunk of persimmon bread. From the glowing ashes of the fire she removed a roasted squirrel, wrapped in steamed corn husks.

"Ah," she said, eyeing her son's fishnet. "You have caught a great big one. Your father will be proud!"

In the field outside Swift Fox's lodge, a nightjar greeted the coming evening.

"That was a real one!" said the boy.

Tecumseh laughed. "Well," he said, "when the real nightjar sings, we know it is late. And time for me to go. Do you think your father will be coming home soon?"

A man poked his head into the lodge. "Swift Fox, you didn't answer me. Didn't you hear the nightjar in the field?"

"This must be the real nightjar!" said Tecumseh. He laughed and extended his hand to Swift Fox's father.

In less than an hour Tecumseh had bought twenty-three horses. As he and his men led the animals back to camp, two nightjars called after them.

CHAPTER 8

The twenty-three black horses carried Tecumseh and his braves south through the gentle rounded hills of the Appalachia. In the warm southlands where Tecumseh traveled, the mountains stayed green much of the year, covered with trees and grasses and wildflowers.

One morning almost three weeks after they'd left Vincennes, Tecumseh called his braves together.

"We are now in the land of the Chickasaw," he said. "It can be dangerous here."

One of his warriors spoke up. "We know the danger, my chief. The Chickasaw are ancient enemies of the Shawnee—and of the Kickapoo as well."

"I see," said Tecumseh. "So the six of you who are Shawnee and the six who are Kickapoo are readying for an attack?"

"We do not want to be caught off guard," said the brave.

Tecumseh became angry. "I do not want any of you to be eager to fight," he said. "We must mend our old wounds with these people. When I was here last, the Chickasaw buried the hatchet. They received me graciously, and I expect they will do the same now.

"The danger I speak of is the bogs," he said. "Places where the ground is soft and spongy. Take care your horses do not get swallowed by them!"

The warriors' horses picked their way carefully through the damp forest, where the air stayed hot, even in the shade. The spruces were more like giant spirits than trees, Tecumseh thought. Mushrooms, capped in tans and yellows and browns, grew in circles around the bases of the trees. Tecumseh pointed out one mushroom. It was as white as snow. "One taste of it," he warned his men, "causes death."

Early one morning, one of the braves woke Tecumseh.

"Many of the men are very sick, my chief," he said. "Eight are faint from the heat. And several more are feverish and swollen with insect bites."

"I will go with you," Black Feather told his cousin. "I have treated such illnesses."

Tecumseh followed the brave and examined the men.

"We will not go on until they are well," he said to Black Feather. "I hope you get them back on their horses in a few days."

*   *   *

Four days later the men were well enough to travel. In some places where they walked their horses, the braves sank to their ankles in the spongy, moss-covered bogs, icy cold with mountain springs. They spoke gently to the startled animals when their hooves broke through the trembling ground. And throughout the bogs, pale pink cranberries, soon to ripen red as blood, grew hidden among the tangles.

At midafternoon the men rode out of the woods into bright steamy sunlight. At a little stream that trickled alongside the woods, they paused to let the horses drink.

Tecumseh sat up straight and shaded his eyes. He looked out beyond the dry grasses, alive with blue asters, purple milkweed blossoms, and bumblebees. On the far side of the open land, a tall palisade of logs fenced in a Chickasaw village. In a field close by the palisade, women with large baskets at their feet were busy harvesting the fall crop of melons and sunflowers, corn and beans.

"It is almost time for *Puskita*, the Chickasaw's Green Corn Festival," said Black Feather, his horse drinking next to Tecumseh's. "A time for a renewal of life—they will put out the old fires, break their worn pottery, and clean the villages.

"It is a good time for us to be here," he said. "The

Green Corn Festival is also the time to end all fighting and forgive enemies!"

"Well," said Tecumseh, "I hope they will feel friendly enough to join our federation. When I was here last, they did not give me their support. Of course, I did not reveal that to Governor Harrison! I led him to believe I have more support than I do. But on this visit, I hope the Chickasaw will realize, if they wish to survive, we all have to stand side by side! The chief in this village is respected by all the Chickasaw. Only if he joins us will the other chiefs follow."

One of the harvesters caught sight of Tecumseh and his braves and called out a warning to her companions. Dropping their baskets, the women ran from the field to the protection of the palisade.

Tecumseh raised his hand to get the attention of his men.

"Listen to what I say!" he said, looking particularly hard at the Shawnee and Kickapoo warriors. "The Chickasaw will soon send a few braves to take a close look at us. Not one of you is to draw an arrow through a bow."

"Are we not to defend ourselves, my chief?" asked the youngest warrior.

"Of course," said Tecumseh. "But we come in peace." The palisade gate opened, and seven men on horseback cantered toward them. "Here they come. Remember what I have told you."

Tecumseh nodded to Black Feather, and, together, they rode out into the meadow to meet the Chickasaw.

"I recognize the brave in the center," Tecumseh said. "He is the son of the chief and is fond of boasting."

When the men were face-to-face, the chief's son spoke first. "Our scouts have been out, watching you make your way through the woods," he said. "I hope the bogs did not frighten you too much?" he asked with a smile.

"If one is prepared for danger," replied Tecumseh, "there is little to fear. It is my wish to meet with your father again."

"I will lead you to him," said the young man.

Tecumseh signaled his warriors to come forward, and the Chickasaw men led their guests to the village.

They rode through the wide palisade gate into a freshly swept open space. The chief's son pointed proudly to the one hundred high-domed dwellings surrounding it. One dwelling had a wall that had blown over. Several women were erecting a new one by stretching woven mats and sheets of bark across tall poles stuck in the ground.

"We are getting ready for the Green Corn Festival,"

the chief's son said with pride. "Come," he added, pointing to a dwelling close by. "My father is waiting for you."

With his heart full of hope, Tecumseh followed the young man.

The Chickasaw chief rose to greet Tecumseh. He was old and bent. His face was creased from a long life in the sun.

"I see you are back, Tecumseh," he said. "Do you still seek members for your federation? On your last visit, some of my warriors were interested, but not enough to join."

"Chief," said Tecumseh, "the time has come for *all* your warriors to unite with us."

The old chief frowned. "And why is that?" he asked. He had known men like Tecumseh—filled with ideas. And some of them not too wise!

"The white men are taking away our land," Tecumseh told him.

The chief frowned for the second time. "Do you not see, Tecumseh, we do not care what is happening up north. The Chickasaw are friends with the white men."

Tecumseh clenched his fists. How could he remain patient with this old fool!

"They may be your friends this day, most respected Chief," Tecumseh said, "but I know, tomorrow they will not be! If you are not united with us, you will be outnumbered. Your people will be driven from their homes like rabbits before a wolf."

The chief grew angry. "The Chickasaw are not frightened rabbits!" he said. "If the white men come, we will not scatter before them. We will fight—and we will win!"

He pushed his way past Tecumseh and flung the door open. "I speak for *all* my warriors," he said. "The Chickasaw will not join you."

"Please, Chief," said Tecumseh, "I did not mean to anger you."

"I accept your apology, Tecumseh," said the chief. "But my people will still not join your federation!"

In the morning Tecumseh and his men left the Chickasaw village behind. They continued the journey farther south toward the land the white men called Alabama and Georgia. As always, Black Feather rode beside his cousin. He sadly shook his head.

"The men are growing disheartened, Tecumseh," he said. "They have traveled so far and have found no new members for the federation."

Tecumseh rode on in silence for several minutes.

"The old chief says his people get along well with the white men," he said at last. "But one day their army will break down his palisade. They will want this land of the Chickasaw—bogs and all!

"I fear the Chickasaw have lived too long near the

bogs," he said. "It is their minds that are trapped in them—trapped in the bogs of ignorance!"

Black Feather smiled. "You are not being fair," he said. "They are not stupid, Tecumseh. They just do not see things your way. They do not see the danger."

Tecumseh shook his head. "Let us both pray we will gain the support of our brothers, the Choctaw and the Creek. If they do not see the danger," he warned, "it will be too late. For the Chickasaw—and for all of us!"

CHAPTER 9

Two weeks later, more than 150 miles north of Tecumseh's party, the weather was cool and breezy in Vincennes. On the lawn next to his house in Indiana, young Benjamin Harrison sat and rolled a ball to his little sister, Mary. Beyond the garden, the older children ran and shouted among fruit trees in the orchard. Upstairs in the nursery, the new baby, Carter, was crying.

Looking down from the council room window, William Henry Harrison watched the road. What was keeping Barron? He paced back and forth across the room and returned to the window in time to see his adviser ride up and dismount. It was about time!

The governor stood behind his desk and waited. He fingered the carvings on the back of the chair and thought of his father. When his father had been governor of Virginia, this chair had been his.

"Sir," said Barron, opening the door, "I got your message to come right away. Is something wrong?"

"Come in, Barron," said the governor, seating himself. "Something has come to my attention that we need to discuss." He waited for his aide to take off his coat.

"Word has come to me through our spies," he said. "By next year, Tecumseh expects to, in his own words, 'lead his people into the Midday.' "

"Midday?" asked Barron.

"Midday," explained the governor, "is the code word for the date his federation will be complete. But I think it means more than that. I think it means that on that day, Tecumseh will attack! Otherwise, why would he say he will *lead his people* into the Midday?"

"Tecumseh is interested in a peace agreement," said Barron.

"It is my belief," said the governor, "that although Tecumseh speaks of peace, he hopes to destroy us! For all we know, he could be gathering up followers by the thousands and heading north at this very minute! If he allies with the British as he threatens, it could prove disastrous. We must not wait until the Midday is upon us! We must act now!"

Barron was astounded. "Do you intend to attack Prophet's Town while Tecumseh is away?"

Governor Harrison shook his head. "We can't attack. We have no cause. That is what I want to discuss with you. I've thought of a way to get *them* to attack *us!* Tell me something about the Prophet. Is he a good warrior?"

"No," said Barron. "That is one of the disgraces of his life. He has never fought in battle. He is said to be a coward."

"Excellent!" said the governor. "That means that Prophet's Town is in the hands of a military incompetent."

"Yes," said Barron. "Although there are skilled warriors with him, the Prophet's in charge."

"Then my plan has a good chance of working," said the governor. "I will gain permission from the secretary of war to set up troops outside Prophet's Town. Then we will wait. If I am a good judge of character, the Prophet will act unwisely and launch a sneak attack. But we will be ready for him."

"Why would he do that?" asked Barron. "The man's a coward."

"He knows he has brave men about him," explained the governor. "He will let them do the work. You see, he thinks he will win!"

The tall windows of the council room glowed rosy in the last light of the setting sun. The governor lit an oil lamp on his desk. While Barron waited, he wrote his letter to Washington. He fixed his seal to the paper and handed it over. "Bring me back a reply as soon as possible."

Alone, Governor Harrison gazed out at the Wabash. He hated war as much as any man, but this spacious land could not be wasted. Why, with the great resources this country had to offer, a great new civilization could be born!

That same night, many miles up the Wabash, the Prophet stood in the light of the round harvest moon. Alone on the little hill outside Prophet's Town, he smiled. It is good to be here without Tecumseh, he thought. Good to be in charge.

He thought angrily of his father and mother who had named him Lalawethika—the Rattle. They said they knew what kind of a boy he'd grow up to be. How could they have known anything? He was only a baby! What boy could hope to become a brave Shawnee hunter or warrior with a name like that?

On frozen days during Tecumseh's ninth winter, his elder brother, Cheesekau, would tell Tecumseh to take off his shirt and swim in the icy river. "Younger Brother," he would tell Tecumseh, "it will help you to become a strong and brave warrior."

When his own ninth winter came, Tenskwatawa had asked Cheesekau, "Should I swim in the icy water so I will turn into a warrior?" Cheesekau had laughed. "You! Little Rattle?" he had said in surprise. "You will never be a warrior. You are too fat and shy. And you don't swim well—you would sink like a stone."

The bitterness of that memory was like a foul taste in his mouth. He would prove himself a great Shawnee warrior. It didn't matter that Tecumseh, the Shawnee chief, had ordered him to keep the peace when he was away. If the time arose, he, Tenskwatawa, the Shawnee Prophet, would command the men into battle!

Pleased with his dreams of power, Tenskwatawa raised his arms above his head and called out to the Great Spirit, the Master of Life.

CHAPTER 10

In the land the white men called Georgia, it drizzled all night. Just before dawn, the weather cleared. Slowly the pale sun rose and warmed the silent village of the Choctaw war chief, Mashuletubbe.

The villagers were asleep on roofed platforms set above the ground on log pillars. The wet roofs of woven grasses and bark kept the sunshine from their eyes.

In one dwelling Tecumseh awoke early. Black Feather, who was lying on a grass mat nearby, had not yet fallen asleep.

"What is the matter, Tecumseh?" he managed to ask. "You have kept me awake all night. You've been tossing like a fish on the sand."

"I have been having a dream," said Tecumseh. "A disturbing one." He looked at his cousin. "I feel something is wrong up north."

"You must not worry so much," said Black Feather. "Be happy that things are going so well here in the land of the Choctaw."

Black Feather stretched out his arm and picked up a small wooden bowl that lay next to Tecumseh. He sniffed it and made a face.

"*Here* is the cause of your dream," he said. "This black drink of roasted leaves that Mashuletubbe gave you; the bowl still reeks of it. It would give bad dreams to any man!"

Tecumseh smiled. "He believes it will strengthen my body and make my mind more powerful for the debate today against Chief Pushmataha."

"Well, it's already done something," said Black Feather. "Because you drank it, I have lost a night of rest!" He rolled over with his back to Tecumseh.

Tecumseh stared at the roof for several minutes. "I hope you are right and there is nothing to fear," he said at last. "But I am deeply troubled. . . ."

Black Feather sighed and rolled back to face Tecumseh. "What was this dream?" he asked.

"In my sleep," answered Tecumseh, "I saw a golden eagle flying to the north. An eagle with wings of silver flew to meet it. They had a terrible fight. With their claws locked together, they whirled higher and higher into the sky. Then, before my eyes, one eagle disappeared. All that was left were its feathers, and they were carried away by the wind. The victorious eagle spread its wings wide and flew straight into the sun, which was at its highest point in the sky. When the bird reached the sun, the world became dark."

"What do you think it means, my cousin?" asked Black Feather.

"I fear that Governor Harrison will fly north to attack Prophet's Town," explained Tecumseh. "My brother Tenskwatawa and he will battle, and one of them will be destroyed."

"In your dream," asked Black Feather, "which eagle won—the golden eagle or the silver eagle?"

"That is the trouble, Black Feather," said Tecumseh. "The birds flew so high, they both looked golden in the bright rays of the sun. I don't know which one prevailed!"

Black Feather stretched and got up from his mat. "Try not to worry too much," he said. "I think it is just the black drink that is giving you this dream.

"And, as I have always told you," he added with a grin, "you are a Cat Man, Tecumseh. You shouldn't get mixed up with birds!" Black Feather patted his stomach. "Let's get something to eat," he suggested. "Being awake all night has made me hungry—for anything but the black drink!"

Tecumseh smiled. "You go," he said. "I would like to be alone this morning. The debate today is very important. It is unfortunate that Chief Pushmataha is my opponent. He does not like the federation, and he is stubborn. But the man is a great public speaker and he has the respect of the old chiefs.

"After you and the men eat, tell them to get ready for their appearance at the debate," he told Black Feather. "See that they dress their hair in scalp locks."

"Scalp locks?" said Black Feather. "They take such time. I know the men will object."

"No matter!" said Tecumseh. "Scalp locks will make them look more impressive." He grinned. "Be content I didn't ask you to do the same!" As soon as Black Feather left to meet with the warriors, Tecumseh strolled to the center of the village and through the large council ring where the debate would take place. Beyond the dwellings, he crossed to a wooded spot and sat on the trunk of an old fallen tree.

In a few hours Choctaw from villages far and near would gather to watch the debate. "I have made sure," Mashuletubbe had said, "there will be a great crowd today!"

Tecumseh nodded to himself. Mashuletubbe was a good supporter. He had sent messengers to the Choctaw chiefs and warriors inviting them to attend the debate. If all the chiefs in the South gave Tecumseh as much support as Mashuletubbe did, the federation would be a success. Perhaps things would work well with the Choctaw!

But Tecumseh's dream worried him. Was it a sign telling him to return to Prophet's Town right away? Or was it simply the black drink playing tricks with his brain? The Choctaw placed such faith in the power of the drink. Maybe, Tecumseh thought, he was seeing clearly just because he had drunk it!

He leaned his head back and closed his eyes. More about the dream was troubling him, but he couldn't figure out what it was.

By late morning the council ring was surrounded by hundreds of warriors. Black Feather found Tecumseh observing the crowd but standing out of their sight.

"My cousin," Black Feather said, "it is time."

Tecumseh looked at his men and Black Feather. They were bare chested and wore dark blue breechcloths. Silver bracelets shone on their upper arms, and flashes of red paint glistened beneath their eyes. Each man had shaved his head except for a strip of thick hair that ended in a braid. The braid, entwined with hawk feathers, hung down between his shoulders.

I was right, Tecumseh thought, the scalp locks make a very good impression. Black Feather handed Tecumseh a red cloth headband embroidered with silver. Except for his hair, the Shawnee chief and his men were dressed alike.

"Let us go now," Tecumseh said to his warriors.

"We must pray that the Great Spirit will guide my words straight to the heart of Chief Pushmataha."

Tecumseh led his men out into the center of the council ring. Mashuletubbe presented Tecumseh and Pushmataha to the audience, and the debate got under way.

"Why should the Choctaw join forces with tribes that have been our ancient enemies?" Pushmataha demanded of Tecumseh. "How do we know they will not attack us in our tepees?"

"My brother," said Tecumseh, "you must forget old hatreds. The only chance for our survival lies with our alliance."

"You are a disturber!" Pushmataha said, pointing his finger at Tecumseh. "My people, the Choctaw, have no reason to fight the white men. Why should we send our fine young warriors to fight in your federation?"

"Not *my* federation—it is *our* federation!" answered Tecumseh. "If we do not all unite as one nation, we will be beaten—one tribe at a time—until there are none!

"You call me a disturber, Pushmataha," he said. "If you do not join me, the white man will do a lot more than disturb you. You will *really* see what a disturbance is!"

Some of the Choctaw warriors laughed. Pushmataha glared at them. "If any of you follow Tecumseh," he

shouted, "I will seek you out and have you killed!"

Tecumseh was shocked. How dare this man threaten others this way! He looked at the old chiefs. Surely they will stop this madman, he thought.

Pushmataha searched the faces in the crowd. "How many of you will join forces with Tecumseh?" he demanded. "Stand up, so I know who you are! It will save me the trouble of finding you!"

Tecumseh was disgusted. He looked at Chief Mashuletubbe. As soon as their eyes met, Mashuletubbe lowered his head. Tecumseh would get no support from the Choctaw.

Tecumseh led his warriors from the village. No one spoke. The only sounds were an occasional birdcall and the clop of horses' hooves.

When the sun was sinking from the sky, Tecumseh broke the silence.

"We will do better with the Creek," he told Black Feather. "I am sure of it. My father once lived among them, and our own mothers have Creek blood flowing in their veins."

"I hope you are right," said Black Feather.

"The Creek have already had trouble with the white men," Tecumseh told him. "They have not had as much trouble as we have had, but enough for them to see the coming danger. The last time I traveled to the South, many Creek were interested in the federation. Let us hope, on this visit, they still feel the same!"

In the community of Tuckabatchee, where the Alabama and Tallapoosa rivers meet, the Creek held a national council for the Shawnee chief.

"Where are the Pequot today? Where are the Narraganset, the Mohican, the Pokanoket?" Tecumseh asked the assembled warriors and chiefs. "Where are these once powerful tribes of our people? I will tell you: They are vanished, swept away by the white men as snow before a summer sun.

"Shall we, without a struggle, give up our homes, our country given to us by the Great Spirit, the graves of our dead?" he cried out. "I know you will shout with me, *Never! Never!*"

But like the Choctaw and the Chickasaw, the old chiefs were afraid to join the federation. Still, one young warrior rose to his feet.

"I wanted to follow you and join your nation," he told Tecumseh. "Now, with the trouble we have had with the white men, I am sure of it!" He raised his fist. "I stand as one with you—a brother." He turned to the crowd. "How many of you stand with me?"

As one, several hundred warriors rose to their feet and raised their fists in the air. For the first time in weeks, Tecumseh felt his heart swell.

An ancient Creek chief struggled to his feet. "Our enthusiastic young warriors do not have the knowledge of their old chiefs," he said. "I speak for my experienced comrades: We are interested in what you have to say, Tecumseh. But before we can give our full support to you, we will send a small band of warriors to Prophet's Town. I want to hear that you have the northern followers that you claim. After my men report back, we will decide if you will get the full support of the Creek people."

"The warriors can go back with me now," Tecumseh said.

The old chief shook his head. "Winter will be soon upon us. They will visit you in the spring."

"But time is short," said Tecumseh.

"In the spring!" said the old chief.

Tecumseh's heart was heavy. He would have to be satisfied with that.

After the council had ended, Tecumseh met briefly with some of the chiefs.

"You look pleased," said Black Feather when his cousin caught up with him later.

Tecumseh smiled. "You know the young warriors who say they are interested in joining our federation, now, on their own? Their excitement may fade by spring. I want them to feel as if they are one of us *today!*"

"How will you do that?" asked Black Feather.

"The chiefs have given their consent for me to hold a ceremony," said Tecumseh. "All the warriors who support us will attend. During the ceremony, each warrior will prepare a number of red sticks for himself. The red sticks, painted with emblems of war, will be symbols of our federation."

"The sticks will remind them of the trip up north in the spring," Black Feather said, nodding approvingly. "They will be more likely to continue their interest." He clapped Tecumseh on the shoulder. "I congratulate you," he said. "It is a splendid idea."

That afternoon, the ceremony was held. Under Tecumseh's direction the warriors cut their own sticks and painted them red.

"These red sticks will be your signs of support for the federation," Tecumseh told them. "They will also bring you luck in battle. From now on, you Creek braves will be called the Red Sticks.

"I look forward to greeting you up north in the spring," he told them. "And soon we will be fighting for our cause, side by side!"

The next morning at dawn, the proud Red Sticks returned with the chiefs to their villages. Not long after, Tecumseh and his men left Tuckabatchee and crossed into the swampy, humid land of southern Alabama.

Late one afternoon a warrior tore into camp.

"My chief!" he called out to Tecumseh. "A great

monster as long as a canoe is attacking Standing Bear!"

Tecumseh and Black Feather leapt to their feet and ran with the warrior to the swamp, where Standing Bear was frantically fending off the snapping jaws of an alligator. He pushed at the alligator with a tree branch. As if the thick branch were a twig, the alligator snapped it in half.

Black Feather leapt forward with his knife. With one powerful downward thrust, he stabbed the alligator through the head, killing it.

Standing Bear struggled to catch his breath. "I am grateful to you, Black Feather," he said. "I was certain the beast would end my life."

Tecumseh smiled at his cousin. "Most impressive," he said. "Who taught you that?"

Black Feather smiled back. "You forget," he said, "I have lived in this land."

The next morning, before they broke camp, Black Feather approached his cousin. "Have you attacked any more alligators?" Tecumseh asked jokingly.

"The men want to go home," said Black Feather. "I am afraid you cannot convince them to stay."

"Nonsense!" said Tecumseh. "What's the matter with them?"

"They are tired," said Black Feather. "And they are sick of the South. These men are from the North, Te-

cumseh, where it is cool. For months they have endured
fever and heat. But now they think the alligator attack
was a sign. They believe they are being warned by the
Great Spirit to leave."

"Call the men together," said Tecumseh.

A short time later the warriors stood in two lines before their chief. In grim-faced silence, Tecumseh paced
in front of them and studied each man's face.

"You are my best men," he said at last. "I am
proud of you. I chose you above all others to accompany
me on this difficult journey. Now that it is getting
rough and dangerous, you wish to abandon our cause and
return home.

"I know that you are suffering. But you are warriors, and warriors are trained to suffer. I am surprised
you are so weak. You know why you are here. We are
here to create an army. You will lose the northern
homes you love if you do not fight for them. And the
fight that you face now is to survive in these unfamiliar
lands.

"Now, which of you wishes to leave?" he asked.

None of the warriors moved.

"Good," said Tecumseh. "We will be on our way at
sunup."

"You work wonders, Cousin," Black Feather said
after the men had left.

"Every man loses heart now and then," said

Tecumseh. He patted Black Feather on the shoulder. "And you, dear Cousin, are here to help me when I lose my own."

Encouraged by the support he seemed to be getting among the Creek, Tecumseh decided not to go straight back to Prophet's Town. He would travel to the open prairie country of the Iowa and Sioux. Perhaps they, too, would join the federation.

On their last night in Alabama, when everyone was almost asleep, a sharp cry pierced the air.

"Did you hear that?" Black Feather asked, poking Tecumseh's side. "Your *unsoma*, the panther, is hunting tonight. It sounds as if he has made a kill!"

Tecumseh couldn't help but smile. In his mind he saw the panther hunting in the moonlight: quietly stalking, then springing through the air with sharp claws, subduing its prey. To hear the panther, his unsoma, in the night was a very good sign. Now he was sure to be successful with the Sioux and Iowa.

Not wanting to disturb the others, Tecumseh spoke in a low voice to Black Feather: "I feel the Great Spirit is with us," he said. "After the Creek warriors visit Prophet's Town in the spring, I am sure we will gain the support of all their people. And then, perhaps, when the Choctaw and Chickasaw hear of it, they will change their mind and join with us as well."

Tecumseh pushed himself up on one elbow and faced

his cousin. "When we get back up north, we have to keep things quiet. There must be no fighting with the white men while we prepare for the Midday.

"When I go to Washington to visit President Madison, I will see if we can reach a peaceful agreement."

Black Feather asked, "What if the white chief will not talk peace?"

"That will not matter," said Tecumseh, "if we have reached Midday. We will defend ourselves, and we will win. Our people will keep their lands, and we will all survive!"

For the first time in many nights, Tecumseh slept well. At dawn he and his men set out once again. They hadn't gone far, however, when one of the warriors pointed ahead to some birds circling in the sky.

"Buzzards," said Black Feather. "The eaters of the dead. Some animal must be *ah-san-wah*, vanished from this life on earth."

As soon as they were close enough to see the dead animal, a low moan rose from Tecumseh's throat. It was the panther. The cry from the night before had not been a cry of triumph but a cry of death!

Tecumseh dismounted to examine the panther. It was unmarked; there were no signs of a fight. What had killed his unsoma? A sound behind a large rock made his spine tingle.

Silently Tecumseh stepped over to the rock and

quickly picked it up. There was the panther's killer—a rattlesnake, his brother—not Tenskwatawa, the Prophet, but Lalawethika, as he had been known for most of his life. Lalawethika, the Rattle.

Tecumseh shut his eyes and tried to keep his body from trembling. He had been such a fool; he should never have trusted his brother. Why hadn't he listened to his dream! He should have gone back to the North right away!

Black Feather came to his side. "I should have listened more carefully to your dream. This is bad luck for all of us."

"We must get back to Prophet's Town without delay," said Tecumseh. But he knew now it didn't matter. It was already too late.

CHAPTER 11

Two miles outside of Prophet's Town a panicked stag scrambled over a high ridge. Two Winnebago braves who had been tracking the animal stopped.

"Red Horse," said one to the other, "let us go back. The great stag will not sacrifice himself for us today."

Red Horse raised his finger to his lips. "Listen, Brave Wolf," he whispered. From a distance, men's voices stirred the air.

The two braves crept to the top of the ridge. They sucked in their breath at the sight before them. An army of white men was stretched across the plain!

They raced back to Prophet's Town to report the news.

"A thousand white soldiers are making camp!" cried Red Horse.

Tenskwatawa was shaken. What should he do now? But then he smiled. Tecumseh, his brother, was miles away. Here was his opportunity to show his good judgment!

"Find out the name of the man in charge," he said to the two warriors.

An hour later Red Horse and Brave Wolf returned with the information. The man in charge was Governor Harrison.

"Tell the governor I wish to meet with him," the Prophet instructed them. But before the men could mount their horses, he called them back.

"I have changed my mind," Tenskwatawa said. "We will fight this army of the white man. After all, what good are talks? Tecumseh never achieved anything at the meetings in Vincennes!"

That night the Prophet called his warriors together in the Tabernacle.

"I have called you here for prayers," he told them. "We must prepare ourselves to fight. We will attack the white army at dawn."

"That is very foolish," objected one warrior. "Many of our warriors are home visiting their villages. We are left with five hundred men. Red Horse says there are twice as many white soldiers."

"No matter what Red Horse says," Tenskwatawa roared, "the white men do not have what you have! You have me—the Prophet—to guide you. I have spoken to the Great Spirit, and he has promised to protect us from harm. He will cover the battlefield with a magical fog. This fog will give you power as you have never known. And at the same time, the white soldiers will be blinded by the fog."

One of the older warriors laughed. "That is nonsense," he said. "There is no magic fog."

Brave Wolf held up his hand. "Listen to me, my brothers," he said. "Tecumseh is our leader. He must have faith in his brother or he wouldn't have left us in his charge. Who are we to say there is no magical fog!"

Another warrior spoke up. "Brave Wolf is right," he said. "The Prophet has shown he has special powers. Before our eyes, did he not darken the sun?"

"I say if we do not follow the Prophet," said another warrior, "Tecumseh will be angry with us."

At dawn Tenskwatawa ordered his men to attack. Clutching his sacred white beans, he climbed the ridge to watch and pray.

The five hundred warriors confidently spread out and, with a bloodcurdling cry, launched their attack. But no magical fog descended to envelop the field.

CHAPTER 12

As Tecumseh and his men traveled north, icy rains pelted their backs and flooded the land. Several times the riders had to wait days before crossing swollen streams. By the time they reached Indiana, it was snowing. Tecumseh had intended to stop and build canoes for the remainder of the trip up the Wabash River, but because it was clogged with large ice chunks the men continued north on horseback. It was late January by the time they finally reached Prophet's Town.

Tecumseh was not prepared for what he saw. The town lay in ruins.

"There is nothing left," said Black Feather. "All the buildings are burned to the ground. Except the Tabernacle. The walls still stand."

"You do not have to tell me, Cousin," said Tecumseh. His voice was shaking. "I have eyes to see."

Huddled at the side of the Tabernacle was his brother.

"Take the men away," he ordered Black Feather. "I wish to see the Prophet alone." He kicked his horse's sides and galloped down the rise into the ruined town. As soon as the Prophet saw his brother coming, he ran to hide inside the building.

Tecumseh jumped from his horse and entered the Tabernacle. Dim rays of sunlight filtered down through its burned-out beams. Tecumseh found Tenskwatawa huddling behind an upturned table.

Tecumseh grabbed him by the hair and yanked him to his feet.

Tenskwatawa tried to cover his face. "Do not kill me," he pleaded. "Do not kill me."

"Look at me," ordered Tecumseh.

Slowly Tenskwatawa raised his head. Tecumseh pulled his brother's face close to his own.

"Because you are my brother, I will let you live," he said. "If you were any other man, you would already be dead." He pushed Tenskwatawa to the ground.

"Let me explain," said the Prophet. "Eight weeks ago Governor Harrison's men arrived and camped two miles away. I thought we could win. So one morning, before dawn, I sent the warriors on charge—"

"You did what?" screamed Tecumseh. "The last

order I gave you was to not fight—under any circumstance!"

The Prophet forced a smile. "We have won," he said. "You see, my dear Tecumseh, we lost but forty braves. The white soldiers lost fifty and we injured more than one hundred."

"And what were you doing when all this was going on?" demanded Tecumseh.

"I stood up on the rise, praying," answered the Prophet.

"Praying instead of fighting," Tecumseh said. "You are still a coward. And still a fool. What has happened to my warriors? Have they been captured by the white men?"

"Do not worry," answered his brother. "They are well. After the battle they returned to their villages to bury their dead. How could I know that the next morning Harrison's soldiers would burn down Prophet's Town?"

Tecumseh's voice was hoarse with anger. "Can you not see, even with your one good eye, what you have done? Do you not see that you have ruined the federation?

"The white man, Governor Harrison, just wanted an excuse to fight us. He was waiting for you to strike the first blow. And he knew that you were stupid enough to do it!" Tecumseh roared. "How can you possibly think you have won? Harrison will declare this an Indian attack and a victory for the white men. He has lost more men, but we have lost everything. Prophet's Town is destroyed, and our followers have left us!"

He leaned down, grabbed Tenskwatawa roughly by his hair, and pulled him to his feet. "Now, get out," he ordered. "Get out before I decide to kill you after all."

The Prophet stumbled away from Tecumseh. He passed through the broken doorway of the Tabernacle and disappeared.

As soon as his brother was gone, Tecumseh put his hands over his face and sank to his knees. All his work had been for nothing, he thought. Word of this would reach the southern tribes. The Creek warriors would never come in the spring.

Tecumseh lowered his hands and leaned back against a fallen beam. If only I had been here just eight weeks ago, he thought. Things might have been different. Now there would be no Midday.

Suddenly his dream became clear! Before everything grew dark, the victorious eagle had flown to the sun. The sun was at its highest point in the sky. It had been Midday! The darkness was a sign that his Midday would never take place.

Through the timbers of the charred roof, Tecumseh gazed to the sky. It was getting dark. Soon it would be very cold. Tecumseh did not feel the winter chill. Inside he felt hollow, empty, filled only with despair. There would be no federation, no nation for his people. How long it would be, Tecumseh could not know. But eventually all their lands would be taken. Then the Shawnee would be like the snowflake in the sun: no more.

A sharp wind whipped the Tabernacle. It was the cold air coming down from Canada. *Canada.* How he had bragged to Harrison about allying with the British army! Now it was almost laughable.

But was it? Perhaps he might still get support from the English. If he could round up his northern warriors, he could take them to Canada. And if war came and the British defeated the Americans, the Shawnee might regain much of their lost land!

Tecumseh got to his feet and searched around the Tabernacle. He found a singed blanket wadded in one corner and wrapped it around himself. He stretched out on the ground.

Lying on his back, his heart filling with hope, Tecumseh fell asleep beneath the shining stars and his father, the sky.

EPILOG

As Tecumseh predicted, his brother's attack on Harrison's troops that chilly November morning ended his hope for an Indian federation. The Battle of Tippecanoe, as that attack came to be called, gave the United States the reason it needed to go on the military offensive against the Indian nation.

Tecumseh, however, promised Harrison that if Great Britain declared war on the United States, he would gather his braves and fight on the side of the English. War was declared in June, eight months after the Battle of Tippecanoe. It came to be known as the War of 1812.

Tecumseh immediately gathered one thousand braves and traveled to Canada, where he joined the British forces as a brigadier general. In battle he distinguished himself as a brilliant and courageous leader. He helped repel an American invasion of Canada and captured the city of Detroit. A little more than a year later, however, in the Battle of the Thames in Canada, Tecumseh was killed by American troops under the leadership of General Harrison. He was about *forty-five years old. Without Tecumseh, the Indian coalition quickly dissolved.*

The Treaty of Ghent ended the war in 1814. Both sides claimed victory. The only real loser was the Native American. For while the war failed to resolve many critical issues between the United States and Great Britain, it did pave the way for further settlement of Indian land by white Americans.

As a result, the Shawnee were forced from their homelands in Ohio and relocated to Oklahoma. Other tribes shared similar fates. In Alabama the Creek rose up in a bloody series of clashes known as the Creek Wars. The Seminole in Florida also rebelled. But like the Creek, they were defeated.

William Henry Harrison became the ninth president of the United States in 1841, in large part due to his popularity as the hero of the Battle of Tippecanoe. He reportedly contracted pneumonia after delivering the longest inauguration speech in American history, however, and died one month later. His grandson Benjamin became president in 1889.

Tenskwatawa—the Prophet—played no significant role after Tippecanoe and died in 1834 in what is now Kansas City.

Though Tecumseh failed in his effort to build a united Indian federation, he will long be remembered as a courageous and intelligent leader who fought—and died—to save his people.